Fashionably Nourished

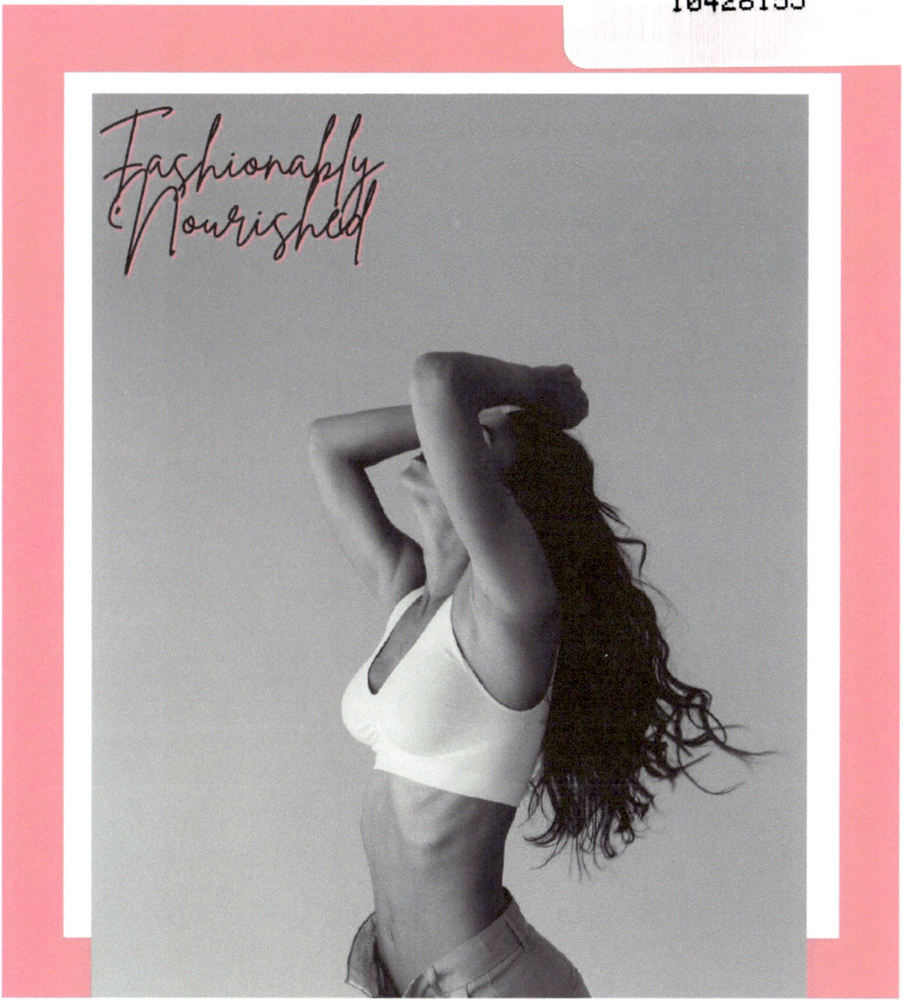

THE RAVISHING TALE OF FASHION

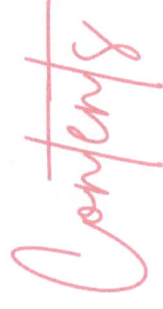

Contents

THE RAVISHING TALE OF FASHION

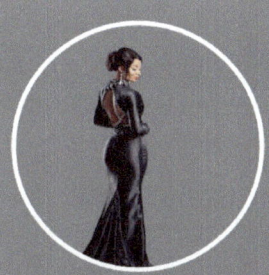

Christabel

ABOUT THE AUTHOR

Fun facts about her:

- Epitomizes the harmonious blend of fashion design finesse, and an adventurous spirit.
- Has passion for both culinary and sartorial excellence.
- A force to be reckoned with in the realms of food, fashion, and beyond.

Contact me on:
abonyichristabel32@gmail.com

WELCOME!

DEAR READER

Christabel is a recent graduate from Nigeria, with a captivating blend of passions that encompass food science, fashion design, and an adventurous spirit. She completed her Bachelor's degree in Food Science and Technology at Nnamdi Azikiwe University, Nigeria, where she honed her expertise and nurtured her passion for the world of culinary exploration.

She isn't just focused on the science of food— she have a natural flair for fashion as well. As a dedicated fashion designer, she crafts unique garments that showcase their creativity and individual style. She draw inspiration from numerous sources, combining her fashion prowess with her knowledge of food science to create truly one-of-a-kind designs that reflect their artistic sensibilities.

Beyond her academic and creative pursuits, she possesses an insatiable wanderlust. She has an innate curiosity that propels her to explore new destinations, immersing herself in cultures far and wide. Whether it's discovering hidden gems in bustling cities or seeking solace amidst the beauty of nature, she thrives on the thrill of new experiences. Her camera serves as a trusted companion, capturing stunning visuals that encapsulate the essence of the places she explore, from the vibrant street fashion to the mouthwatering culinary delights.

While her journey has roots in Nigeria, her aspirations branch out towards the world's fashion capitals, where she seek to further her understanding of global fashion trends and immerse herself in the creative whirlwind that defines these cities. Her desire is to witness firsthand the fashion-forward cultures that thrive in metropolises around the world, ignites her imagination and fuels her hunger for growth and exploration.

Christabel
Abonyi

THE RAVISHING TALE OF FASHION

3

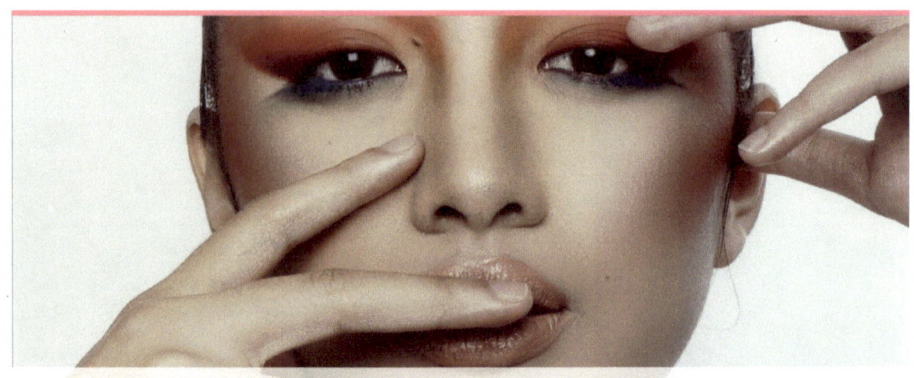

AIMS AND OBJECTIVES

To inspire readers with creative fashion and food concepts, offering new and interesting ideas they can incorporate into their own lives while providing entertainment and enjoyment to readers by presenting visually appealing fashion photos or mouthwatering food images thereby educating and informing them about all there is to know about food and fashion trends.

Section
TWO

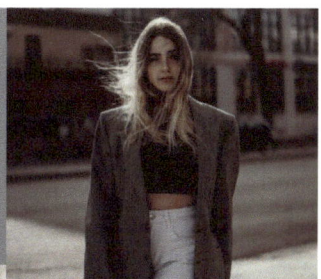

A FASHIONISTA

We all have a similar idea of the basics of a fashionista. Someone that is interested in fashion, probably to the extent that the person's life revolves around the subject. From there though, I think we all have different definitions. Perhaps a fashionista is someone like the character Rihanna in her everyday life who is always bold with her designer clothes, and embodies it with her unique styles.

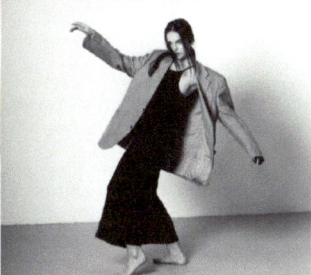

Others would say that a fashionista doesn't follow trends but creates her own fashion path which in turn becomes a trend, while some would say it's a trend follower to the core. Others would say, someone who promotes high fashion and who is purely obsessed with fashion. So no doubt there are different ideas of a fashionista.

A Fashionista is an individual who is passionate about fashion and has a deep appreciation for style and trends. They are known for their keen sense of fashion and their ability to effortlessly put together stylish and unique outfits. Here's everything you need to know about a Fashionista:

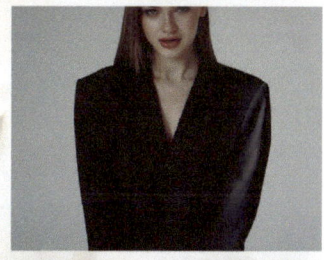

"Because there is always a passcode to every outfit" - Christabel Abonyi

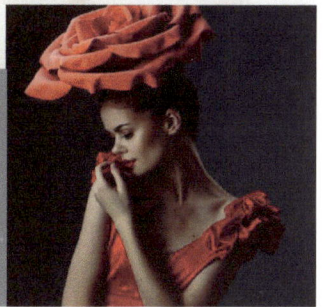

1 *Fashion Sense*: A Fashionista possesses a natural inclination towards fashion and always stays updated with the latest trends. They have a good eye for aesthetics, understanding how clothes, accessories, and makeup can come together to create a cohesive and fashionable look.

2 *Personal Style*: Fashionistas often have a distinctive personal style that sets them apart. They are not afraid to experiment with different fashion elements, mix patterns and textures, and incorporate unique pieces into their wardrobe. Their style may vary, ranging from classic and elegant to edgy and avant-garde.

3 *Trendsetter*: Fashionistas are trendsetters and influencers in the fashion industry. They have a knack for spotting up-and-coming trends and aren't afraid to try them before they become mainstream. Others often look to Fashionistas for inspiration and guidance on what's hot and trendy.

4 *Confidence*: Fashionistas exude confidence in their fashion choices. They believe that style is an expression of one's personality and use fashion as a medium to showcase their individuality. They don't shy away from attention and are comfortable being the center of attraction.

5 Fashion Knowledge: A Fashionista possesses extensive knowledge about fashion history, designers, and key fashion moments. They keep themselves updated on fashion news, runway shows, and the latest collections from both established and emerging designers.

6 *Creativity*: Fashionistas have a creative flair and are known for their ability to combine different elements to create unique and eye-catching outfits. They are skilled at layering, accessorizing, and mixing unexpected pieces to create a fashion-forward look.

7 *Inspiration*: Fashionistas draw inspiration from various sources such as music, art, culture, street style, and nature. They are constantly seeking inspiration to further enhance their fashion sense and inject fresh ideas into their outfits.

8 *Fashion Influence*: Fashionistas often have a strong social media presence and can be influential figures in the fashion industry. They may have fashion blogs, Instagram accounts, or YouTube channels where they share their style tips, fashion finds, and inspire others with their fashion choices.

9 *Shopping Savvy*: Fashionistas are skilled shoppers who know where to find the best deals, upcoming sales, and hidden gems. They have a talent for scouting unique and stylish pieces, whether in high-end boutiques, vintage stores, or thrift shops.

10 *Passion for Fashion*: Above all, Fashionistas have an immense passion for fashion. They truly enjoy the artistry and creativity that comes with dressing and expressing themselves through clothing. Their love for fashion permeates all aspects of their lives and drives them to constantly evolve and explore new fashion territories.

"You can have anything you want in life if you dress for it." - Edith Head

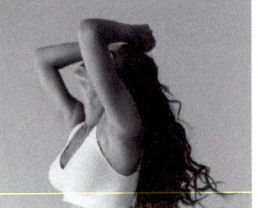

ATTIRE ON THE RUNWAY

Being a Fashionista is not about following trends blindly but rather about finding your unique style and expressing yourself through fashion. Embrace your individuality and have fun exploring the world of fashion!

A fashionista's wardrobe is versatile and filled with a variety of clothing options for different occasions. Here are some essential clothing pieces a fashionista might have for various events:

1 *Casual/Everyday wear*:
Jeans: A staple in any wardrobe, jeans come in various cuts and styles.
T-shirts: Basic tees or graphic tees can be paired with different bottoms.
Blouses: Feminine blouses in different fabrics and patterns add versatility.
Sweaters: Lightweight and chunky sweaters for cooler weather or layering.
Dresses: Comfortable and stylish dresses in different lengths and styles.

2 *Formal/Professional wear*:
Blazers/Jackets: Structured blazers or tailored jackets instantly elevate an outfit.
Dress pants: A well-fitting pair of trousers in neutral colors is essential.
Pencil skirts: Versatile and classic, pencil skirts create a polished look.
Button-up shirts: Crisp, tailored shirts add a professional touch.
Sheath dresses: Figure-flattering, knee-length dresses for formal occasions.

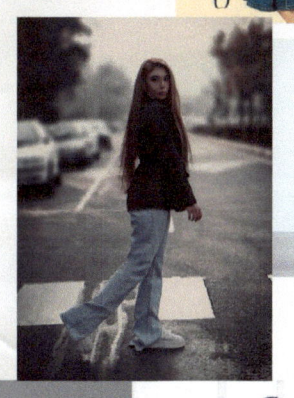
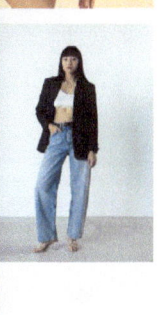
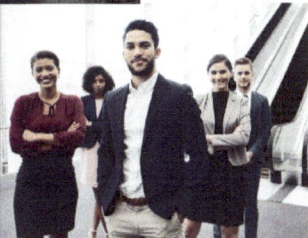

"FASHION is 30 percent clothing and 70 percent ATTITUDE"

African native prints: For glamorous events, sparkly outfits which makes a big statement!

3 *Evening/Party wear:*
Cocktail dress: A semi-formal dress that hits above or just at the knee.
Statement tops: Unique and eye-catching tops paired with tailored bottoms or skirts.
Jumpsuits: Trendy and modern, jumpsuits offer a sleek alternative to dresses.
African native prints: For glamorous events, sparkly outfits which makes a big statement.

4 *Beach/Resort wear:*
Swimsuits: Various styles like bikinis, one-pieces, or tankinis for beach outings.
Cover-ups: Lightweight and flowing cover-ups to wear over swimsuits.
Maxi dresses: Comfortable, flowy dresses ideal for beach or resort wear.
Wide-brimmed hats: Stylish and functional accessories to protect from the sun.
Sandals/Flip-flops: Comfortable footwear for beach or poolside lounging.

A fashionista is more democratic than designer clothes, brands and labels! someone who doesn't have a lot of money and can't afford designer items could still consider themselves a fashionista, it all goes down to having a sense of style naturally.
Some people can literally create unique styles out of nothing and make it look like a million bucks.

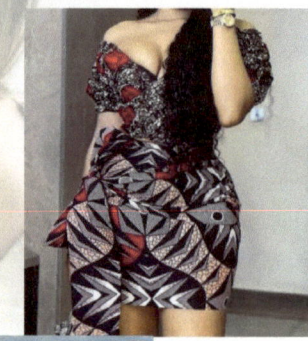

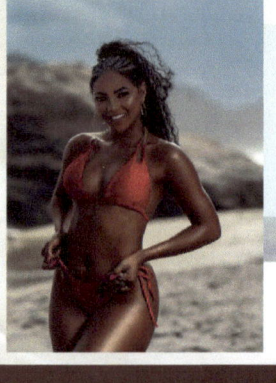

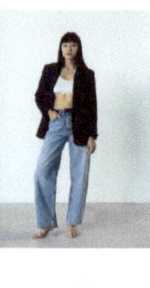

When it comes to fashion, I want to see individuality-Rihanna

EXPLORING THE RELATIONSHIP

FASHION AND FOOD

The relationship between fashion and food is multifaceted and often intertwined. Both fashion and food are forms of creative expression deeply ingrained in our daily lives and cultural identities. Ultimately, both industries share a creative spirit, cultural significance, and a desire to engage and inspire individuals, making their relationship an intriguing intersection of art, culture, and personal expression. Here are a few facets of the relationship between fashion and food:

1 *Aesthetics and Presentation*: Just like fashion, food is often judged by its appearance and presentation. Both industries value aesthetics and the art of presentation. From haute cuisine plating techniques to Instagram-worthy food trends, there is often a conscious effort to make food visually appealing and to evoke desire, similar to fashion's emphasis on stylish and visually appealing clothing.

2 *Cultural Signifiers*: Both fashion and food are cultural signifiers. They reflect and communicate identities, values, and traditions. Traditional clothing and traditional cuisines are often deeply rooted in cultural heritage, conveying stories and symbolizing cultural belonging.

3 *Trends and Influences*: Like fashion, food experiences trends and shifts in popular taste. Food trends can influence fashion, and vice versa. For instance, the rise in popularity of health-conscious eating has led to athleisure and activewear becoming fashion staples. On the other hand, fashion can inspire food trends, such as the emergence of color-coordinated cafes or fashion-themed desserts.

4 *Collaboration and Cross-Promotion*: Fashion and food often collaborate and cross-promote. Fashion designers have partnered with restaurants and food brands to create limited-edition collaborations, such as designer-branded packaging, menu items, or exclusive fashion-themed dining experiences. This synergy allows both industries to tap into each other's audiences and create unique, cross-disciplinary experiences.

5 *Branding and Lifestyle*: Fashion and food brands often aim to create a lifestyle around their products. They market not just products but a particular aesthetic and experience. Luxury fashion houses, for example, may offer branded restaurants or cafes as extensions of their brand, creating a complete immersive experience for consumers to engage with their brand values.

To fully embrace the fusion of fashion and food, one can take several steps to integrate these two creative realms.

This is about creativity, the key is to approach both fashion and food with an open mind, explore their connections, and discover unique ways to intertwine them in your own personal style and experiences. Here are some ways to embrace this fusion:

1 *Food Styling Experiment* : Approach food preparation and presentation with a fashion-forward mindset. Consider color coordination, texture pairing, and aesthetic plating techniques to make your culinary creations visually striking and fashionable. Think beyond taste and explore the visual aspect of food.

2 *Fashion-Inspired Tablespaces*: Create table settings and tablespaces that draw inspiration from fashion aesthetics. Incorporate elements like fabrics, patterns, and colors that resonate with your favorite fashion styles or designers. Use stylish tableware, linens, and decorations to create a visually cohesive and fashionable dining experience.

3 *Culinary-inspired Fashion Choices*: Seek fashion pieces or accessories that feature culinary motifs or themes. Look for clothing, jewelry, or accessories with food-related prints, patterns, or designs. Opt for garments with unique textures or materials that reference food, like sequins resembling sprinkles or fabric with prints of iconic ingredients or dishes

4 *Host Fashion-Food Events*: Arrange gatherings or events that celebrate the fusion of fashion and food. Host fashion shows where models wear outfits inspired by different cuisines or specific ingredients. Organize pop-up shops with food tastings, or collaborate with local fashion and food businesses to create immersive experiences where attendees can enjoy both aspects simultaneously.

5 *Attend Fashion-Food Collaborative Events*: Keep an eye out for events that merge fashion and food. Look for runway shows that incorporate food elements into their presentations, or attend pop-up events where chefs collaborate with fashion designers to create unique culinary experiences. These events offer the opportunity to witness the fusion firsthand and engage with both fashion and food in a dynamic setting.

10

7. Document Your Journey: Use social media or start a blog to share your exploration of the fusion of fashion and food. Document your culinary experiments, fashion choices, event attendance, and creative collaborations. This allows you to inspire others, connect with like-minded individuals, and contribute to the growing conversation around this exciting fusion.

QUICK AND STYLISH MEALS FOR BUSY FASHIONISTAS

As a fashionista, it is important to prioritize both style and health.
Here are some healthy meal ideas that are delicious, nourishing, and could align well with a fashionable lifestyle:

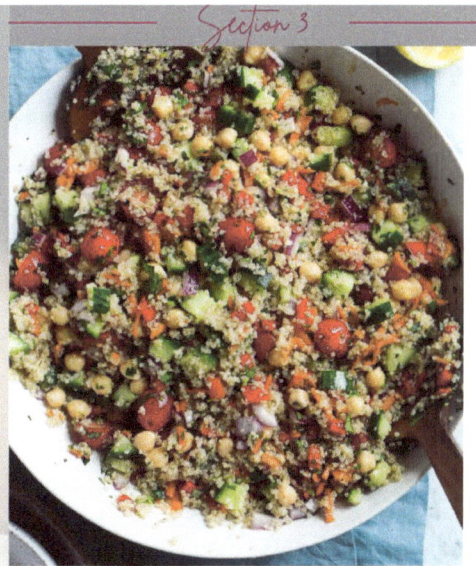

1 *Quinoa and Vegetable Salad*: Mix cooked quinoa with a variety of colorful vegetables like cherry tomatoes, cucumber, bell peppers, and avocado. Add fresh herbs, lemon juice, and a drizzle of olive oil for a flavorful and nutritious salad.

2 *Buddha Bowl*: Build a bowl with a base of mixed greens or brown rice, and top it with roasted vegetables like sweet potatoes, Brussels sprouts, and broccoli. Add a protein source like grilled chicken, tofu, or chickpeas. Drizzle with a homemade dressing made with olive oil, lemon juice, and tahini.

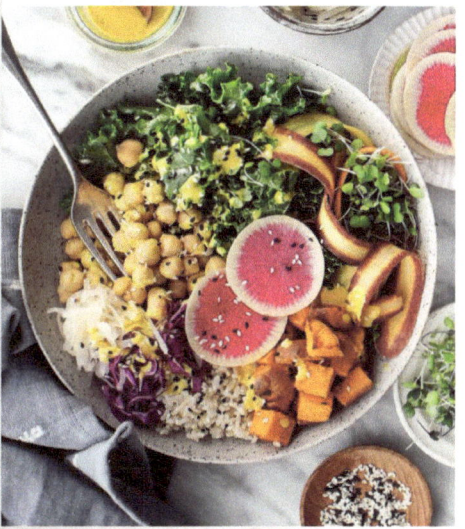

THE RAVISHING TALE OF FASHION

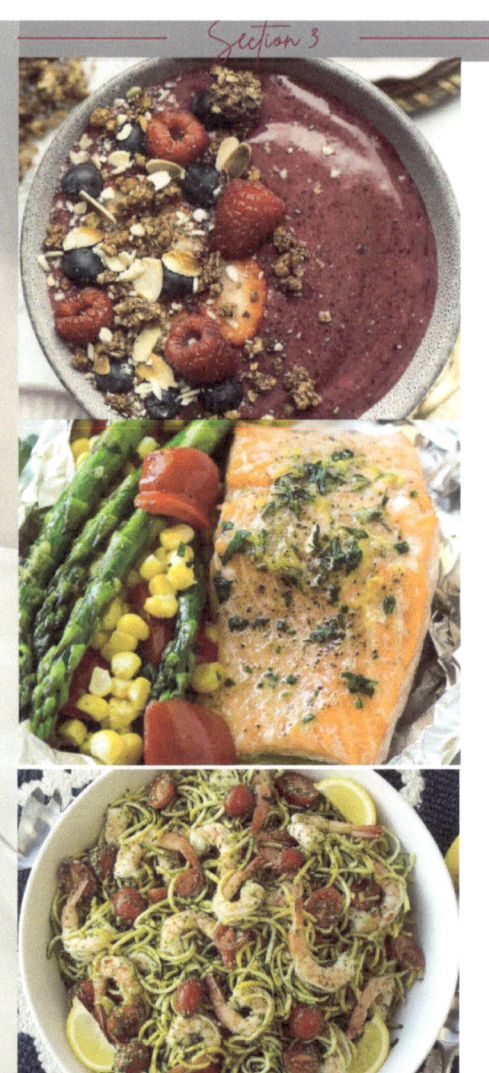

8 *Smoothie Bowl*: Blend together frozen fruits like berries, banana, and spinach, along with a liquid base like almond milk or coconut water. Top your smoothie bowl with granola, chia seeds, sliced fresh fruit, and a dollop of almond butter for added nutrient density.

4 *Grilled Salmon with Roasted Vegetables*: Marinate a salmon fillet in a mix of lemon juice, olive oil, garlic, and herbs. Grill the salmon until cooked through and serve it alongside a colorful medley of roasted vegetables like carrots, zucchini, and bell peppers.

5 *Zucchini Noodles with Pesto and Grilled Shrimp*: Spiralize zucchini into noodles and toss them with homemade pesto sauce made with basil, pine nuts, garlic, and olive oil. Grill some shrimp to add a lean protein component and serve it over the zucchini noodles.

6 *Nigerian Jollof rice*: Nigerian jollof is a beloved and iconic dish that represents the rich culinary heritage of Nigeria. This flavorful rice dish is widely regarded as one of the nation's most famous and delicious recipes.

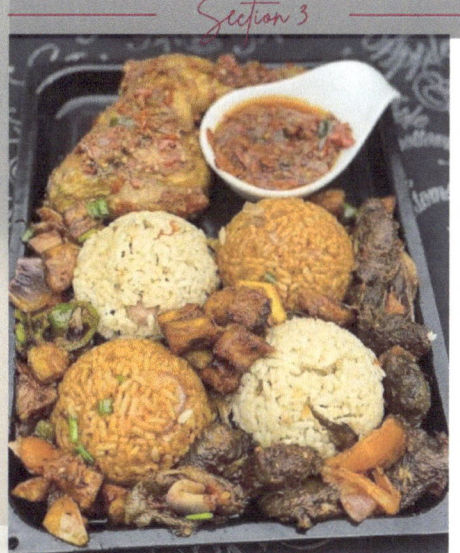

Known for its vibrant red color. It is cooked by combining parboiled rice with a flavorful blend of tomato purée, fried onions, and peppers. The dish is generously seasoned with spices such as thyme, curry powder, and garlic powder. It is often prepared with an assortment of vegetables, such as carrots, peas, and bell peppers, to add texture and additional nutritional value. It is not just a meal, it is a symbol of unity, celebration, and community.

Nigerian Jollof rice has gained a global reputation and has even sparked friendly culinary debates about its superiority among various West African countries. Its popularity has spread beyond Nigeria, and it is now loved and appreciated by food enthusiasts all over the world. Nigerian Jollof rice serves as a representation of Nigeria's vibrant culinary scene and its ability to create delicious and culturally significant dishes.

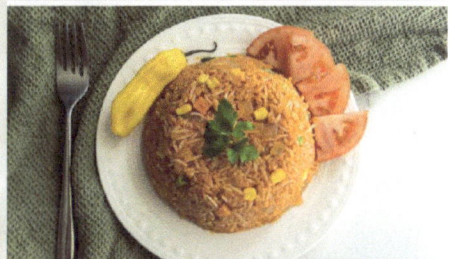

Remember to always prioritize balance and moderation, as well as listening to your body's individual needs and preferences. These meal ideas provide a starting point for creating healthy, delicious, and fashionable meals that are both satisfying and nourishing.

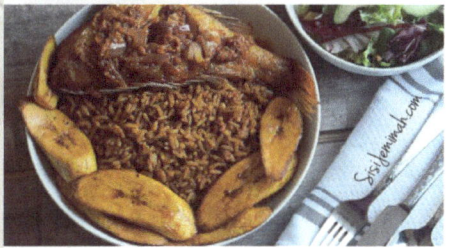

WHEN FASHION COLLIDES

When fashion collides with life, it can have various outcomes and impacts depending on the circumstances. Here are a few possibilities:

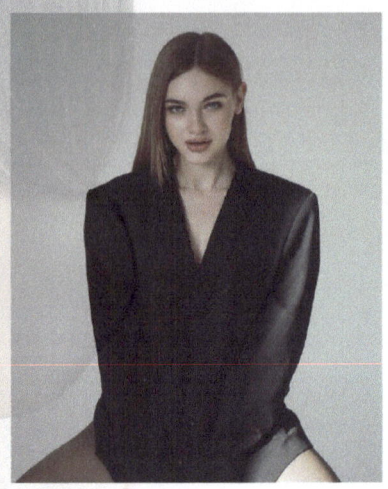

1 *Self-expression and identity*: Fashion can play a significant role in how individuals express themselves and define their identities. When fashion collides with life, it allows people to showcase their personality, style, and creativity. Fashion becomes a vehicle for self-expression, helping individuals communicate who they are to the world.

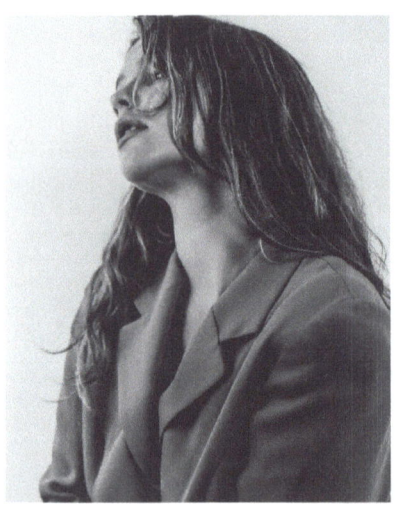

2 *Cultural and societal influences*: Fashion often reflects and responds to cultural and societal influences. When fashion collides with life, it can mirror social and cultural changes or challenge societal norms. Fashion designers and brands might incorporate elements of cultural diversity, environmental awareness, body positivity, or inclusivity, sparking important conversations and promoting social progress.

3 *Confidence and empowerment*: Fashion has the power to boost confidence and empower individuals by allowing them to present themselves in a way that aligns with their aspirations. When fashion collides with life, it can help people feel more confident, express their inner selves, and assert their individuality.

Wearing clothes and accessories that make them feel good can positively impact their self-esteem and overall well-being.

4 *Trends and consumerism*: Fashion collisions with life often involve following or setting trends. Fashion trends constantly evolve, driven by influential designers, celebrities, social media, and popular culture. As fashion influences our lives, it can lead to consumerism, as individuals seek to keep up with the latest trends and constantly update their wardrobes. This can have both economic and environmental consequences

5 *Creativity and innovation*: When fashion collides with life, it fosters creativity and innovation.

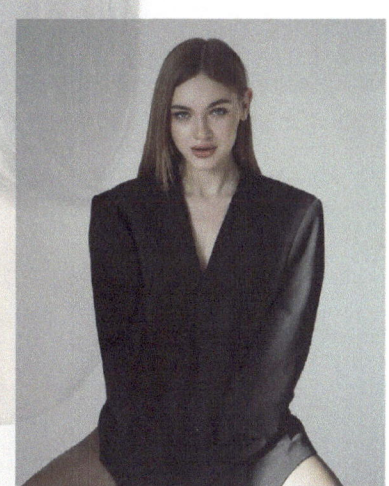

Fashion designers, stylists, and influencers continuously experiment with new materials, silhouettes, colors, and combinations, pushing the boundaries of what is considered fashionable.
This creativity contributes to the evolution of fashion and inspires others to think outside the box.

It is important to recognize that fashion is subjective and means different things to different people. When fashion collides with life, it is a reflection of personal choices, cultural dynamics, and the broader social context. The impact of this collision can be diverse, ranging from self-expression and empowerment to societal change and consumer behavior.

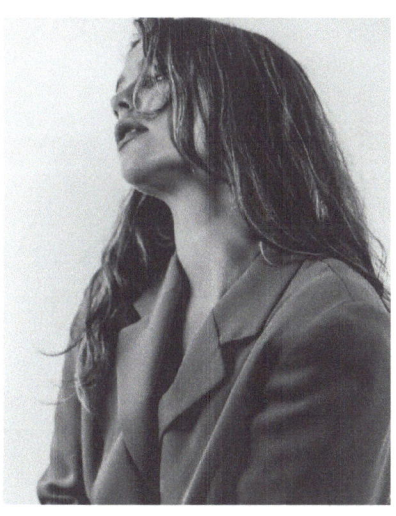

DRESSING FOR FOOD PHOTOGRAPHY

A good photographer is as important as a good fashionista. I mean, showing up will not be complete without the glams and pictures and posting on your social media pages.

Food is pretty, but sometimes it needs some help. Here's a list of tricks that I have gathered and can be used every day.

1 *Water in a red wine*
Red wine in a shoot is always a challenge. It looks red to us emotionally, but it usually translates to a dark black hole in an image. So when you use a red wine in a shoot, you can blend it with water in a different bottle until it's light enough to see through, capturing a true red on the camera.

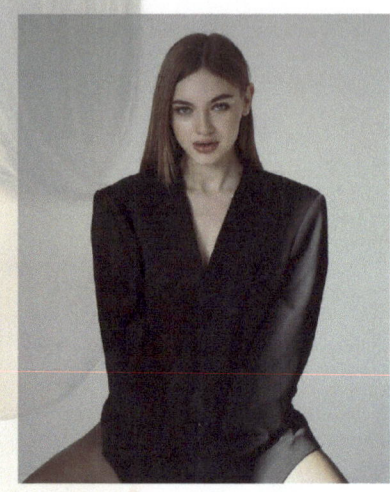

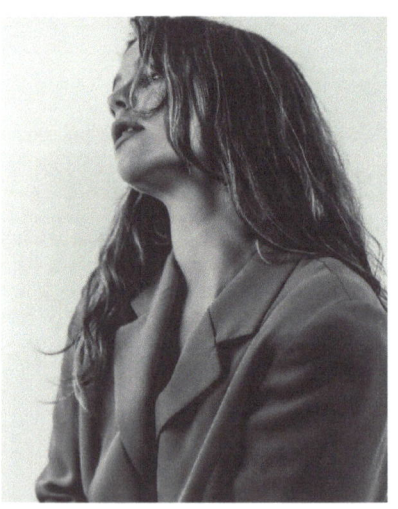

2 *Undercook meals turns out great*
Most meals looks great when they are undercooked and are able to maintain their shape and color by just wilting them with steam. The camera darkens charred edges, so broil all your food a few shades lighter than you would eat it.

3 *Styling a dish is best served cold*
Very few foods need to be shot hot, most actually they look better styled cold. The exceptions are editorial shoots in restaurants.

4 Display *the salad naked*
Think of salads as flower arranging on a plate. Heavy dressings will almost always weigh down your greens or make them look wilted and stale. No matter what the salad —style it naked. If it has a dressing that needs to be showcased.

⑤ *Small dishes are the best dishes*

It's very challenging to style and shoot on a large dinner plate. Food shooting is an exercise and less is more. A small selection of perfectly placed items on a smaller plate read more bountiful than a mass of correctly portioned food on a large plate.

When prepping food for a photo shoot, it's important to know your style and the audience.
Blog followers will demand more authenticity but require less perfection. A package shoot requires more perfection. Magazines require food that is styled and propped to such an artistic aspirational delight we just want to linger on the page a little longer.

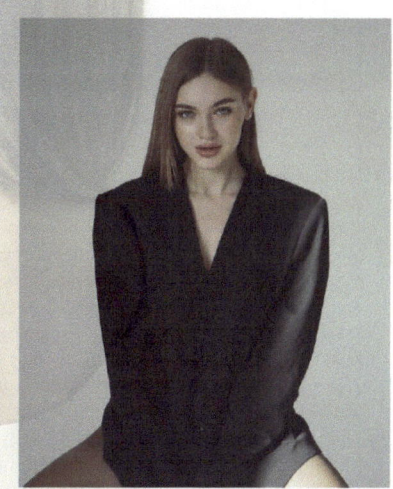

On social, it's all about texture and color and surprise. If it's interesting, it's shareable. In essence, styling is about really seeing food, it's more sculpture and storytelling than cooking and I think that is what makes it so much fun.

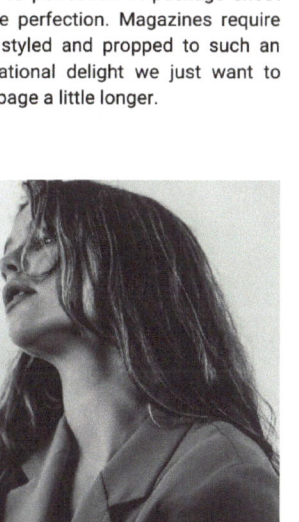

RUNWAY TO THE KITCHEN

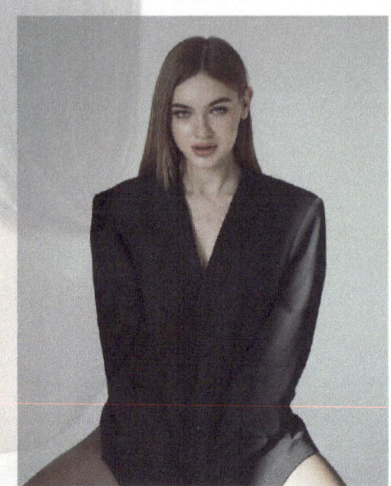

"Runways to the Kitchen" serves as a celebration of the intersection between food and fashion, elevating the dining experience to new heights. It offers chefs an opportunity to channel their creativity, challenge culinary norms, and present dishes as visual masterpieces. This concept adds an extra layer of excitement and entertainment to the dining experience, transforming a meal into an immersive and memorable event.

This idea revolves around the idea of transforming the kitchen into a stage for culinary performances, where chefs become performers and the dishes they create become artistic presentations.

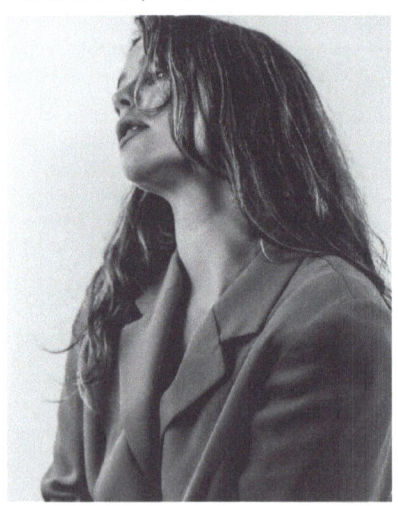

Let's delve deeper into the concept of "Runways to the Kitchen.

❶ *Fusion of Creativity*: "Runways to the Kitchen" merges the creative worlds of fashion and culinary arts, allowing chefs to explore their artistic capabilities beyond the mere act of cooking. It encourages them to think like designers, incorporating elements of color, texture, and composition to present dishes that resemble works of art.

❷ *Elevated Dining Experience*: By incorporating elements from fashion shows, "Runways to the Kitchen" events aim to offer diners a premium and unforgettable dining experience. The visually appealing presentation, storytelling aspect, and interactive engagement with the chef add an extra layer of excitement and entertainment to the meal.

RUNWAY TO THE KITCHEN

3 *Storytelling Through Food*: Similar to fashion designs telling a story on the runway, the dishes prepared in a "Runways to the Kitchen" event tell a narrative. Chefs take inspiration from various sources, such as cultural heritage, personal experiences, or current trends, to create dishes that convey meaning, evoke emotions, and engage diners on a deeper level.

4 *Influencing Food Trends*: The fusion of food and fashion in "Runways to the Kitchen" can also influence culinary trends and the food industry as a whole.

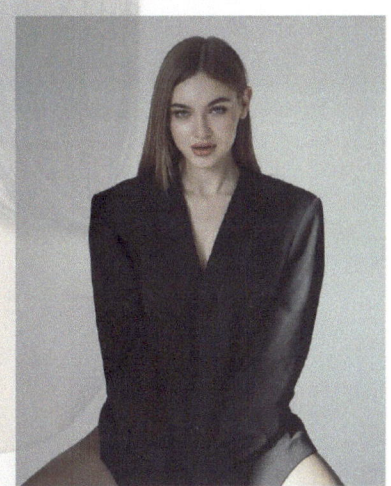

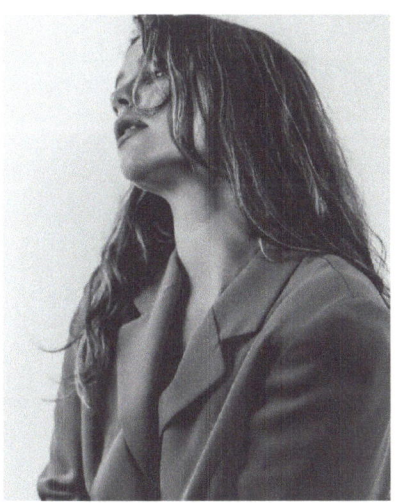

Just as fashion trends set the tone for style and design, the creative and visually captivating presentations in these events can inspire chefs and restaurateurs worldwide to innovate, experiment, and elevate their own culinary offerings.

5 *Social Media Appeal*: Given the visually stimulating nature of "Runways to the Kitchen," these events have the potential to create captivating content for social media platforms. Diners often share photographs and videos of the beautifully presented dishes, amplifying the reach and impact of the event. This can lead to increased exposure for the chefs and restaurants involved, as well as the promotion of culinary and fashion artistry.

FASHION-INSPIRED TRENDS

Fashion fades, but style is eternal - Yves Saint Laurent

Here are some fashion-inspired trends that have gained popularity through social media platforms:

1 *Influencer Fashion*: Social media influencers play a crucial role in shaping fashion trends. Influencers with large followings often showcase their outfits, styling tips, and fashion discoveries, influencing their followers' fashion choices and preferences.

2 *#OOTD*: The hashtag #OOTD, meaning "Outfit of the Day," has become immensely popular on platforms like Instagram. Users share daily outfit posts, showcasing their personal style and inspiring others. These posts often include fashion pieces, accessories, and styling ideas.

3 *DIY Fashion*: Social media platforms have facilitated the rise of DIY (Do-It-Yourself) fashion trends. Users share creative ideas for upcycling and customizing clothing items, giving them a unique and personalized touch.

DIY fashion content provides inspiration for repurposing old garments or transforming thrifted finds into trendy and fashionable pieces.

4 *Fashion Hauls*: Fashion hauls, where users share videos or images of their recent shopping finds, have become popular on platforms like YouTube and Instagram. These videos feature individuals showcasing their purchases, trying them on, and providing reviews or styling tips. Fashion hauls serve as inspiration for others, introducing new brands, styles, and fashion-forward pieces.

5 *Fashion Challenges*: Social media challenges, such as the "7 Days, 7 Outfits Challenge" or "One Piece, Multiple Ways Challenge," encourage users to showcase their creativity in styling outfits. These challenges not only promote sustainable fashion by encouraging users to mix and match existing pieces but also create a sense of community and engagement within the fashion community, and the list continues.

FASHION-INSPIRED CITIES

Paris offers endless opportunities for fashion enthusiasts.

Here are some fashionable destinations that a fashionista might enjoy visiting:

1 *Paris, France*: Known as the fashion capital of the world, Paris offers endless opportunities for fashion enthusiasts. Explore the iconic Champs-Élysées, visit high-end designer boutiques, and admire the collections at world-renowned fashion houses like Chanel and Dior. Don't forget to visit the famous department stores like Galeries Lafayette and Le Bon Marché.

.

2 *Milan, Italy*: Milan is another fashion-forward city that is home to renowned designers and fashion houses. The city is famous for its luxury shopping streets, including Via Montenapoleone and Via della Spiga. Milan also hosts Fashion Week twice a year, where you can catch runway shows and immerse yourself in the latest trends.

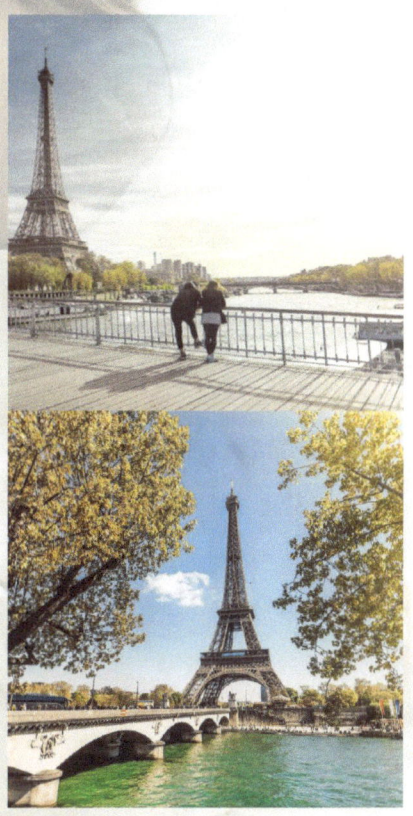

3 *New York City, USA*: As a vibrant fashion hub, New York City offers a mix of high-end fashion, street style, and emerging designers. Explore the trendy neighborhoods of SoHo and the Meatpacking District, visit iconic department stores like Bergdorf Goodman and Saks Fifth Avenue, and attend fashion events like New York Fashion Week or the Costume Institute Gala at the Metropolitan Museum of Art.

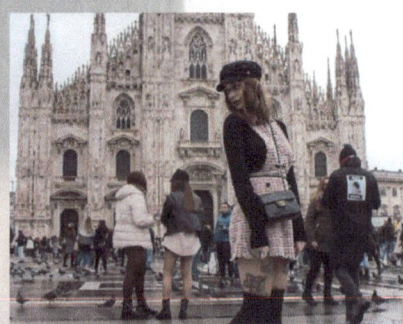

4 *Tokyo, Japan*: Tokyo has a unique and vibrant fashion scene that combines tradition with modern trends. Explore the trendy districts of Shibuya and Harajuku, known for their street style and quirky fashion boutiques. Visit flagship stores of Japanese fashion brands like Comme des Garçons and Issey Miyake, and check out fashion-forward shopping centers such as Omotesando Hills.

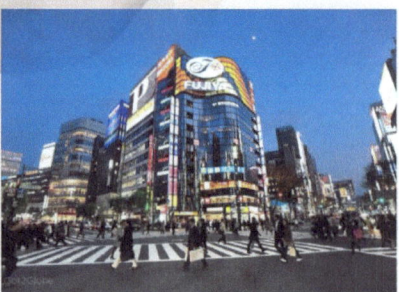

5 *London, UK*: London is renowned for its eclectic and innovative fashion scene. Explore the stylish streets of Bond Street and Mayfair, visit iconic department stores like Selfridges and Liberty, and browse the cutting-edge designs at fashion spaces like Dover Street Market. Attend London Fashion Week for a firsthand experience of the city's fashion buzz.

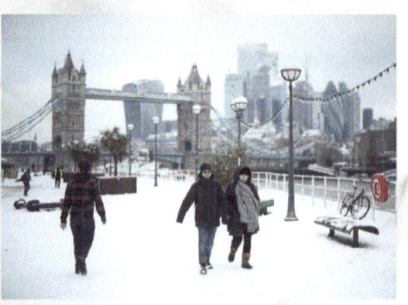

6 *Seoul, South Korea*: South Korea's capital, Seoul, has become a fashion hotspot in recent years. Discover the latest Korean fashion trends in trendy neighborhoods like Myeongdong and Hongdae. Visit multi-brand fashion concept stores like Boon The Shop, explore the fashion-forward area of Gangnam, and don't miss out on attending Seoul Fashion Week.

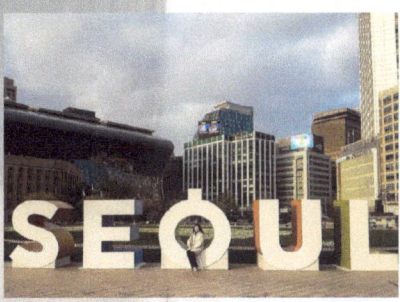

7 *Lagos, Nigeria*: Lagos State in Nigeria is undeniably beautiful, as it captures the essence of the country's vibrant culture, rich history, and diverse natural landscapes. It is a place where tradition meets modernity, and where bustling city life coexists with stunning beaches and awe-inspiring landmarks. This city is often referred to as the fashion capital of Nigeria and has gained recognition on the global fashion stage.

Lagos State is home to a multitude of talented fashion designers who have gained recognition both nationally and internationally. From renowned designers such as Deola Sagoe and Mai Atafo to emerging talents like Lisa Folawiyo and Orange Culture, the fashion scene in Lagos is fueled by creativity and innovation. These designers draw inspiration from the rich cultural heritage of Nigeria and blend it with contemporary designs to create stunning collections that are worn globally.

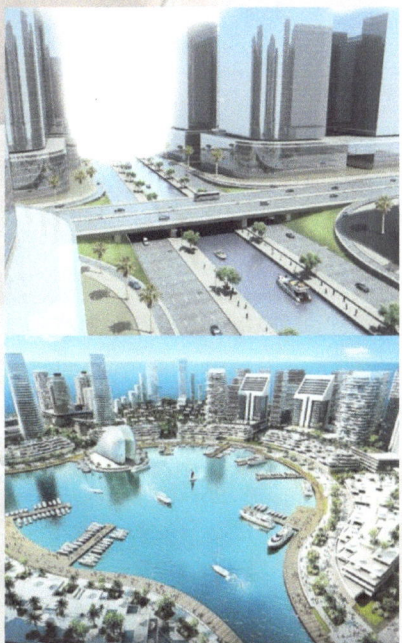

Lagos, Nigeria

THE RAVISHING TALE OF FASHION

FASHION QUOTES

Key takeaways

- "If you like it gorgeous then wear it."
- "Fashion is like eating, you shouldn't stick to the same menu." - Kenzo Takada
- "You can have anything you want in life if you dress for it." - Edith Head
- "Fashion is the armor to survive the reality of everyday life." - Bill Cunningham
- "Its not about brand, its about style."

THE RAVISHING TALE OF FASHION

"

Great personal style is an extreme curiosity about yourself
- Iris Apfel

Fashion is the armor to survive the reality of everyday life
- Bill Cunningham

We say something every morning when we decide how to dress
- Alison Lurie

"

"

A girl should be two things: classy and fabulous

- Coco Chanel

Clothes aren't going to change the world, the women who wear them will

- Anne Klien

When you don't dress like everybody else, you don't have to think like everybody else.

"

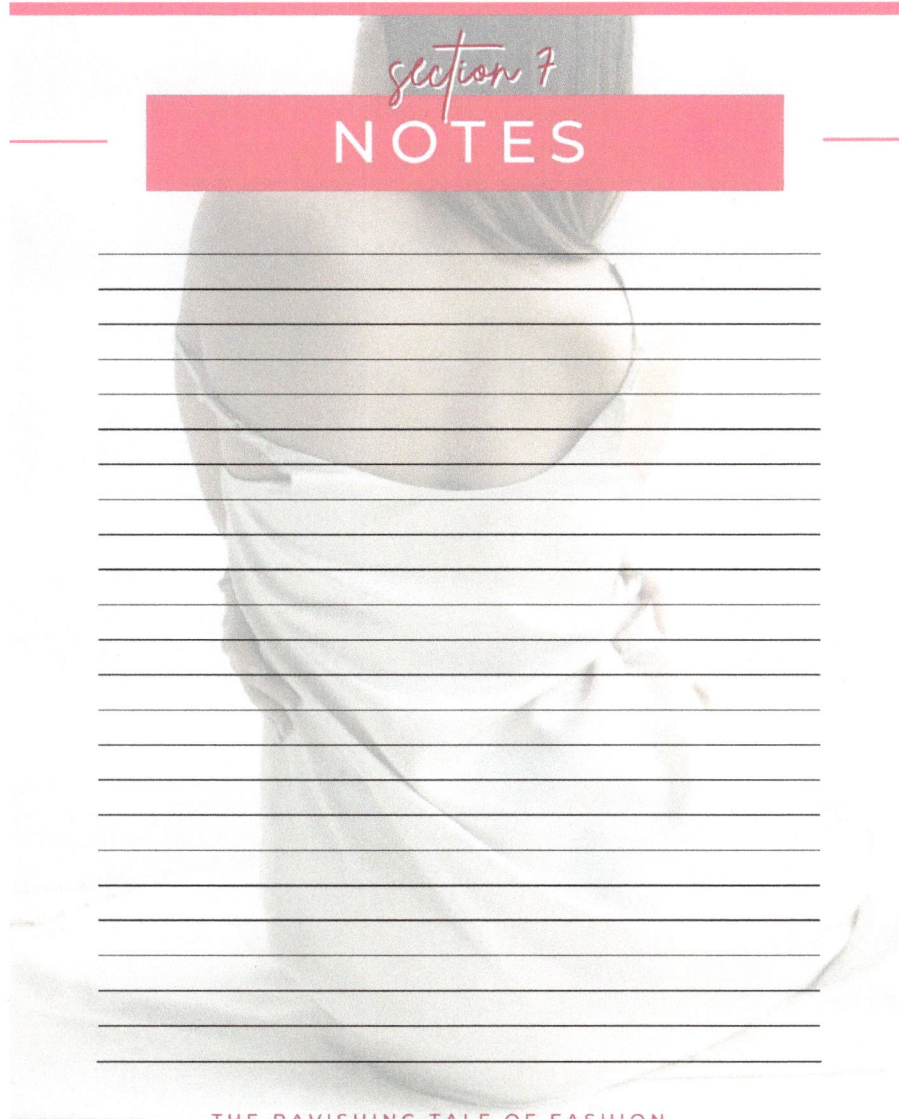

section 7
NOTES

_____
_____
_____
_____
_____
_____
_____
_____
_____
_____
_____
_____
_____
_____
_____
_____
_____
_____
_____
_____
_____
_____
_____
_____
_____
_____
_____
_____

THE RAVISHING TALE OF FASHION

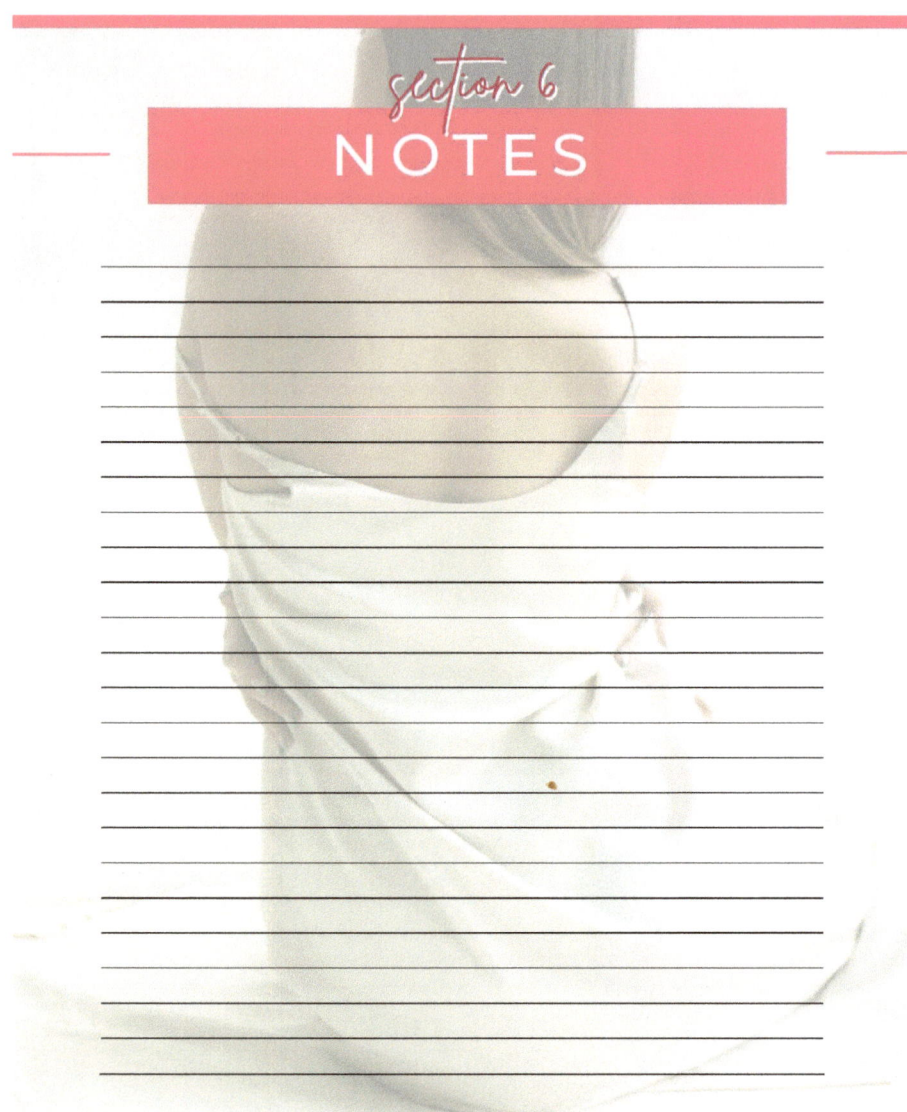

section 6
NOTES

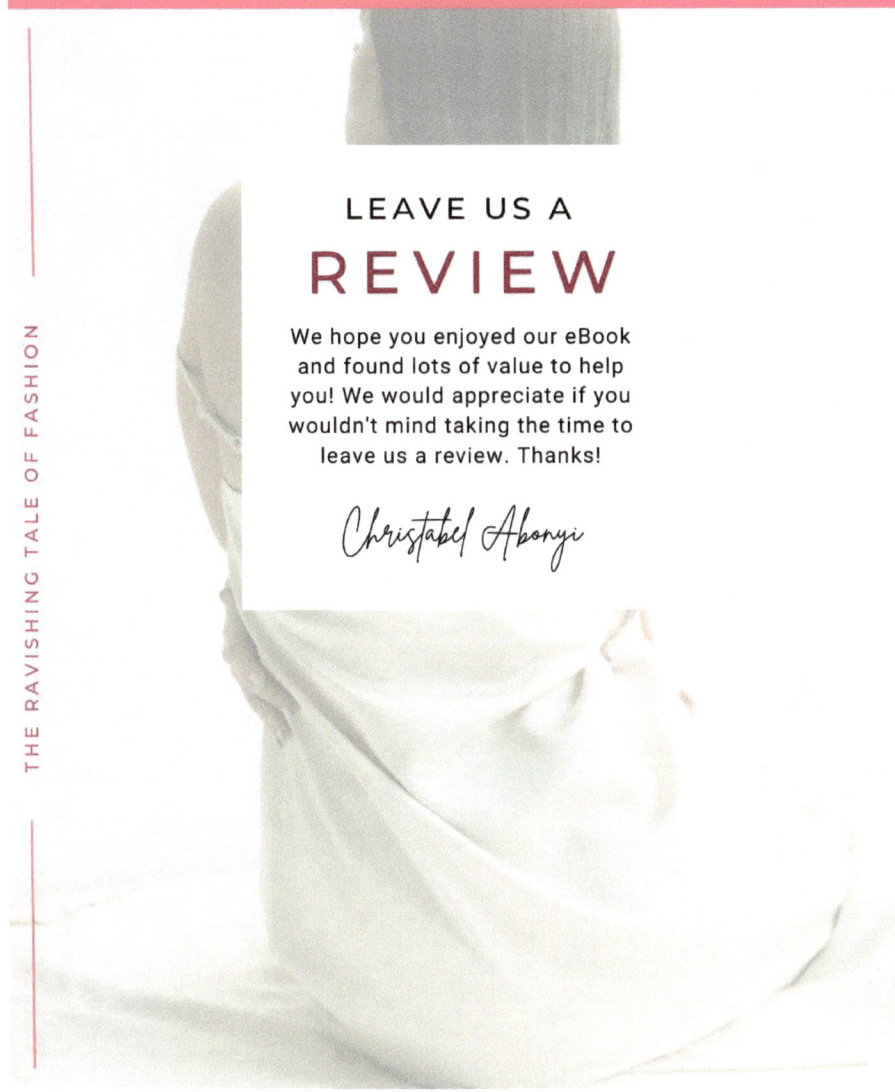

LEAVE US A
REVIEW

We hope you enjoyed our eBook and found lots of value to help you! We would appreciate if you wouldn't mind taking the time to leave us a review. Thanks!

Christabel Abonyi

THANK YOU FOR YOUR FEEDBACK!

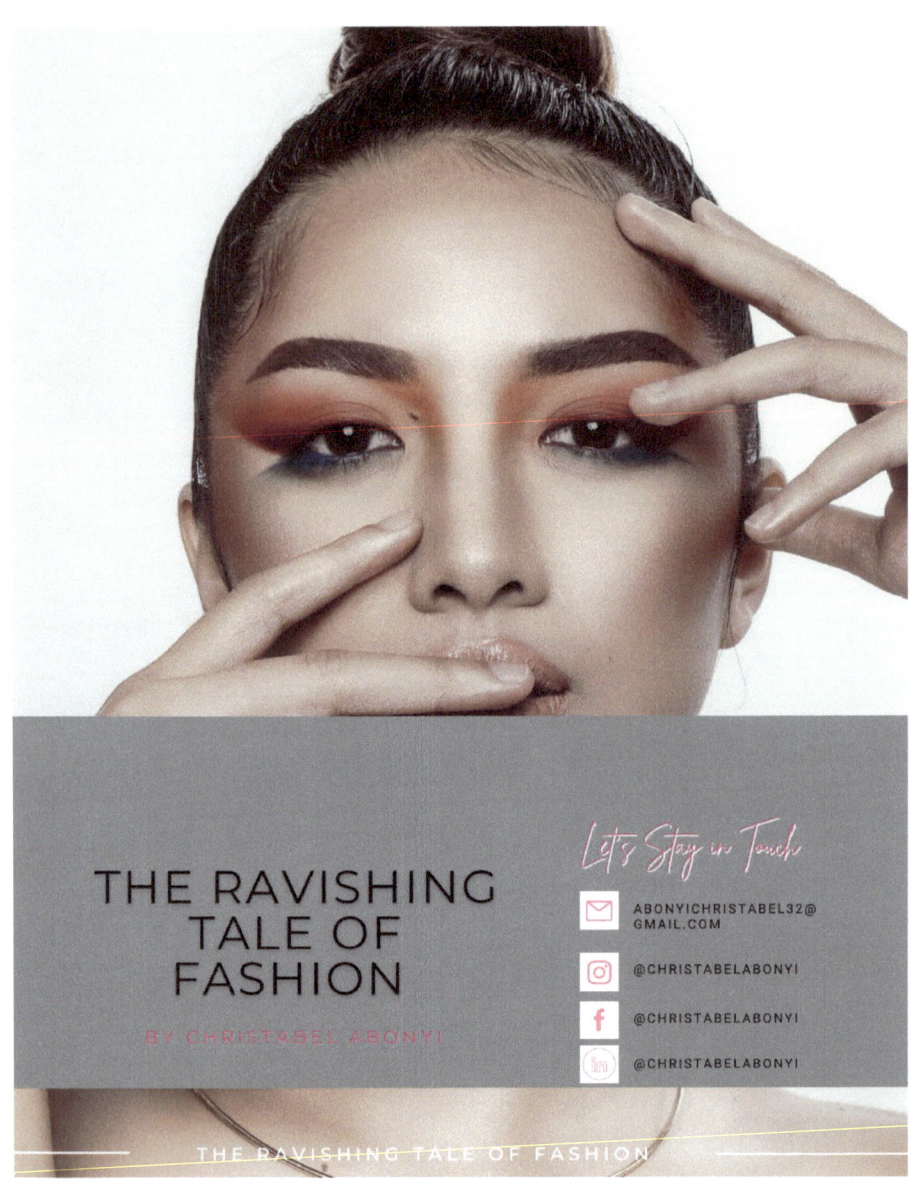

THE RAVISHING TALE OF FASHION

BY CHRISTABEL ABONYI

Let's Stay in Touch

ABONYICHRISTABEL32@GMAIL.COM

@CHRISTABELABONYI

@CHRISTABELABONYI

@CHRISTABELABONYI

www.ingramcontent.com/pod-product-compliance
Lightning Source LLC
Chambersburg PA
CBHW040327010626
45792CB00024B/2262